Pebble® Plus

SEA LIFE

REGAL TANGS

by **Mari Schuh**

Raintree is an imprint of Capstone Global Library Limited, a company incorporated in England and Wales having its registered office at 7 Pilgrim Street, London, EC4V 6LB – Registered company number: 6695582

www.raintree.co.uk
myorders@raintree.co.uk

Editorial Credits
Elizabeth R. Johnson, editor; Aruna Rangarajan, designer;
Kelly Garvin, media researcher; Tori Abraham, production specialist

ISBN 978 1 4747 0477 9 (hardcover)
19 18 17 16 15
10 9 8 7 6 5 4 3 2 1

ISBN 978 1 4747 0482 3 (paperback)
20 19 18 17 16
10 9 8 7 6 5 4 3 2 1

British Library Cataloguing in Publication Data
A full catalogue record for this book is available from the British Library.

Photo Credits
Alamy/Roberto Nistri, 21; Dreamstime/Lukas Blazek, 5, Glow Images/ImageBROKER, 17; iStockphoto/mirecca, 15; Shutterstock: artefacti, 8, bluehand, cover, Brad Barkel, 9, Dobermaraner, 13, Godruma, cover (background), Johanna Goodyear, 11, Peter Leahy, 19; Superstock/imageBROKER, 7

Design Elements: Shutterstock: SusIO, Vectomart

Printed and bound in China.

Contents

What is a regal tang?

Regal tangs have a secret. Sharp spines pop out from their tails when they are attacked. These fish are also called surgeonfish.

spine

Regal tangs have many names.
They are called palette surgeonfish,
Pacific blue tangs and hippo tangs.

Regal tangs live in the Indian
and Pacific oceans.
They swim in warm water
near coral reefs.

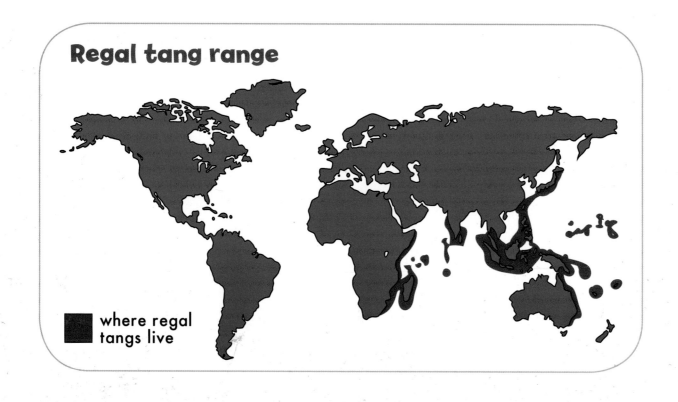

Regal tang range

■ where regal
tangs live

Up close

Regal tangs are oval-shaped.

They have flat bodies.

They can grow to

30 centimetres long.

Regal tangs are bright blue
with black markings.
Small scales cover their bodies.
Their tails are yellow.

Finding food

Regal tangs often eat together
in small groups.
They use their sharp teeth to
pick algae off of rocks and coral.

Growing up

Regal tangs hatch from their
eggs after about one day.
The larvae grow quickly.
After one week, scales form
on their bodies.

Young regal tangs are yellow.
They turn blue as they get older.
Regal tangs live for up to
30 years in the wild.

Staying safe

Regal tangs hide to try to stay safe. They use their spines if they are attacked. These beautiful fish can defend themselves.

Glossary

algae small plants without roots or stems that grow in water

coral reef type of land close to the surface of the sea made up of the hardened bodies of corals; corals are small, colourful sea creatures

defend protect something or someone from harm

hatch break out of an egg

larva animal at the stage of development between an egg and an adult; more than one larva are larvae

scale one of the small, thin plates that cover the bodies of fish

spine hard, sharp, pointed growth on an animal's body

Read more

Living or Non-living in the Ocean (Is it Living or Non-Living?), Rebecca Rissman (Raintree, 2014)

Pacific Ocean (Oceans of the World), Louise Spilsbury (Raintree, 2015)

Usborne First Encyclopedia of Seas and Oceans, Jane Chisholm (Usborne Publishing, 2011)

Websites

www.bbc.co.uk/nature/habitats/Reef
Learn more about coral reefs and the creatures that live in them.

www.national-aquarium.co.uk/50-fun-facts
Fun facts about sea and ocean life.

Index